EVIE KIEHLE

Where are the Women?

A Simple Guide to the Under-Representation of Women in American Politics, Its Causes, Its Consequences, and What You Can Do

To Abby, Addison, Genevieve and my mom. Thank you for supporting this crazy idea of mine.

Contents

Foreword

I was first introduced to this topic in a Sociology class I took during my junior year of high school. I found myself fascinated by this topic and spent the next few months learning everything I could. I wanted to gather everything I'd learned into something tangible, something others could read and learn from. That is the purpose of this book.

This book is for everyone - middle school, high school, college students, parents, grandparents, and even politicians. I wrote this book to be accessible so it doesn't go into intense detail. I highly encourage readers to, if interested, look into these topics in more depth. I would also like to thank everyone who is reading this book right now. Thank you.

1

The Under-Representation of Women in American Politics

The United States has come far regarding the representation of women in politics. Women gained the right to vote in 1920 with the passage of the Nineteenth Amendment; the first woman in Congress, Jeanette Rankin, was elected in 1917; the first woman on the Supreme Court, Sandra Day O'Connor, took the seat in 1981; a woman, Hillary Clinton, was a primary candidate for president in 2016; and a woman, Kamala Harris, became the vice president of the United States for the first time in 2021.[1]

Yet, while America has made significant progress since its founding, women are not equally represented in American politics. Women represent 51% of the United State's population,[2] but as of July 2023, only 28.8% of the House of Representatives and only 25% of the Senate are women.[3] Even though the U.S. came close when Hillary Clinton won the popular vote in 2016, our country has never had a female president in the 234 years the position has existed.[4]

Currently, the United States is ranked 71st in the world in regard to the percentage of women in national legislatures, meaning that a substantial number of countries have more women in office than we do.[5] Even countries that we (the U.S.) perceive as more historically or culturally patriarchal than ourselves have higher percentages of women in their governments and have or have had female heads of state.[6]

The under-representation of women in political office is evident, but the reasons why, as well as the consequences of this under-representation, are much more complex. The government's primary role is to create and enforce policy that represents and supports the will and well-being of the public. The absence of women in political roles can lead the needs, concerns, and voices of women - over half the population - to be overlooked. [7]

The United States is a diverse country, but our elected officials do not represent this diversity. Our representatives are elected to *represent* our country, including our diversity. So why don't they? There is an assumption that this lack of diversity is primarily due to voter bias, but it is actually due to who chooses to run for office in the first place.[8] As political scientists Jennifer Lawless and Richard Fox note in their 2022 report, *The Gender Gap in Political Ambition*, "When women run for office, they perform just as well as men - they raise just as much money, win just as many votes, and claim victory just as often." [9] The under-representation of women in political positions is not primarily due to voter biases but rather to a gender gap in political ambition.[10] *Women are less likely than men to run for political office.*

In general, young Americans - ages 13 to 25 - have lower political ambition than previous generations, with young girls and women having the lowest levels.[11] This is concerning, as the health of a democracy is partially measured by how willing its citizens are to engage in the political system, whether by voting or running for elective office. If the majority of young Americans do not express interest in running for office, with young women least likely to express interest, this implies that our democracy is unhealthy.[12]

There are many reasons for the gender gap in political ambition, and this book will only aim to address and discuss some of the most prominent ones. The next chapter will detail why young Americans have low levels of political ambition and what this means for American democracy. The following chapter will dive into the phenomena behind the gender gap in political ambition. The final chapter will highlight potential solutions that parents, schools, our political system, and young Americans themselves can implement to combat low political ambition, amend the gender gap, and ensure the equal representation of women in politics.

2

The Low Political Ambition of America's Youth

A healthy democracy requires a large number of citizens who are willing to engage and participate politically by running for office. There are more than 500,000 elected positions in the United States, from the president, the vice president, senators, congressional representatives, state governors, state legislators, city officials, and mayors to school board members.[13] To successfully function and accurately represent the people, our country requires a large number of people, especially young people, to be willing to step up to the plate and run for elective office.

Unfortunately for America, this is not the case. The majority of young Americans, from teenagers to college students, have no interest in a candidacy at any point in their lives, be it at any level of government.[14] *Young people have low political ambition.* Political ambition is one's desire to run for political office.[15] Only about 11% of young people have *seriously* considered running for office, while over 60% have *never* considered it.[16] Not everybody needs to express an interest in holding political office, as that would be neither productive nor possible, but when levels of political ambition are *this* low, there is cause to be concerned for the well-being of our democracy.

Now, it is not as though young people do not have the desire to create positive change in the world because that desire *is* present. Young people care about current political and economic issues [17] and want to make a meaningful difference in their communities and the world around them.[18] However, young people do not see politics as a way to do so, resulting in low levels of political ambition.

Political ambition is not something one is born with. It is malleable, it is subject to change.[19] Political ambition is based on one's political socialization, the process in which people gradually develop political ideas, beliefs, and attitudes as they age.[20] Political socialization occurs through political exposure, exposure to politics from the media, the home, school, and through peers.[21] Political exposure forms a person's perception of the government, which creates an individual's cost-benefit analysis of the risks and rewards associated with a political candidacy.[22] People have low political ambition when the costs of running for office outweigh the benefits, resulting in a phenomenon that political science professor Shauna L. Shames calls "candidate deterrence." [23]

The Cost-Benefit Analysis of a Political Candidacy

Every person forms a different cost-benefit analysis of the risks and rewards of pursuing a political position based on their own experiences and encounters. While there are several commonly identified risks and rewards, the impact each has on one's political ambition differs from person to person. Commonly identified costs are campaign finances, loss of time, loss of privacy, job insecurity, having to deal with the media, the possibility of facing negativity from the media and other politicians, and political polarization.[24] The most common rewards are the opportunities that politics can provide - the opportunity to solve problems, the opportunity to be a leader, the opportunity to assist communities and individuals, the opportunity to work with a wide variety of people, and the opportunity to make a difference.[25]

While the impact of each cost or benefit varies for each individual, some costs and benefits are significantly more influential on political ambition. The most overwhelming cost is the financial costs of a political candidacy, with the idea of asking for money particularly unappealing.[26] The most influential reward is the belief that politics are an effective method of creating positive change.[27] When one believes they can use politics to solve problems and create meaningful change, their levels of political ambition increase so dramatically that one can potentially overlook the costs of running.[28]

Young People's Perceptions of the Political System

Unfortunately, the majority of young people believe politics are ineffective.[29] An individual's cost-benefit analysis depends on that individual's perception of the government as a system. The policy passed, the political climate, the behavior of politicians, the nature of political media, and one's exposure to the political system all play a role in shaping one's perceptions.[30] Young people do not perceive politics as an effective or efficient method of creating change.

A Tufts University survey conducted after the 2022 election

revealed that less than a third of young people, ages 18 to 29, trust the two major political parties, state governments, prominent news sources, Congress, or the president.[31] These results aren't surprising. Negative views of the government are widespread, and citizens' trust in government is at historic lows.[32] This general distrust of government has many factors, but it can be traced back mainly to the Reagan era of politics when politicians began running "against" the government.[33] In this political strategy, the government is painted as the enemy, and the candidate is presented as a savior who will clean up or fix the government if elected. Since Reagan, this strategy has become the norm, and while it may work occasionally, it creates a distrust of the government in the minds of the public.

Nowadays, this strategy doesn't seem to work as well as it did. Nowadays, politicians are held in low regard, far from being the heroes and role models of the previous generations. Nowadays, the public sees politicians as power-hungry, dishonest, and immoral - willing to do anything for re-election.[34] Many Americans view the political system as broken and corrupt, failing to accomplish anything from policy to compromise.[35] And these views are understandable.

The past two decades of politics have been messy. Campaigns have become more and more negative, less about a candidate's merits and more about the faults of their opponents. Scandals are widespread. Extremity has been rising, dangerously rearing its ugly head during the January 6th insurrection, a violent attack on the U.S. Capitol Building that led to countless injuries, immense monetary damages, and even five deaths.[36] Congress has been passing fewer and fewer laws, with the 112th Congress, active from 2011 to 2013, being the least productive Congress since the 1800s.[37] With a political climate rife with scandal, conflict, gridlock, negative campaigns, and irresponsible behavior from politicians, it's no wonder that politics leave a bad taste in many young people's minds.

The behavior of politicians and the climate of the current political arena only play one role in establishing one's perception of the government, as exposure to politics through the media, the childhood home, school, and peers is the primary groundwork for one's political perception.

Young people's political perception is greatly affected by their low levels of political exposure. Political ideas and interests stem from political exposure in the childhood home, but political ambition is absent in the modern family.[38] On the rare occasions when politics *are* mentioned, they are spoken about negatively, mockingly, and distastefully, suggesting that our political system is broken and corrupt. And while most families emphasize the importance of voting, they don't encourage much else regarding political involvement - whether that be protesting, contacting representatives, or running for office.[39] In fact, from the way their parents discuss (or don't discuss) politics, many young people believe their parents would rather they pursue any career other than a political one.[40] This fact is especially concerning for their political ambition, as those who receive encouragement from their parents to run for office are five times more likely to consider running for office.[41] If young people, people easily impacted by the beliefs of their parents, are not being encouraged to run for office and feel as though their parents would disapprove of them running for office, they will not run.

A lack of political exposure in other aspects of daily life also causes low political ambition. Politics - civics, history, and government - are taught in many schools, but there is little political encouragement from teachers or the curriculum.[42] The majority of young people avoid regularly discussing politics with their friends, viewing politics as too negative and dividing for civil conversation.[43] Young people also consume less traditional political media than the generations before them.[44] When they do consume traditional news sources, they are often confronted with polarizing, negative, and outright biased news coverage that focuses excessively on conflict and scandal rather than any policy passed.[45] *On the whole, young people and even not-so-young people see politics as too polarizing, too ineffective, and too pointless to bother keeping up with at all.*

Why does political exposure matter so much? If the political system is indeed broken, how could exposure to its faults impact political ambition? It may be surprising, but there is a chance that political exposure can combat the negative perceptions stemming from the behavior of politicians, the lack of compromise, and the lack of policy passage. It has been shown that "when young people are deeply immersed in politics, they push through their initial revulsion and see ways to contribute." [46] Unfortunately, few young people expose themselves or are exposed to politics due to the polarizing nature of our current political system.

Political Polarization

Political polarization is the convergence of political attitudes and ideas toward ideological extremes, away from the center.[47] Political polarization has increased rapidly since 2000, reaching an all-time high in the past decade.[48] One side's win is always the other side's loss.[49] Members of one political party are expected and encouraged to have intense negative emotions toward the other party.[50]

Some divisiveness is natural and even necessary in a democracy [51], but these extreme levels of polarization have serious consequences. Political polarization leads to policy gridlock that harms government institutions and results in the passage of fewer and fewer laws.[52] As Jesse Shapiro, a political economy professor at Brown University, notes, "When people in different political camps cease to respect each other, it's harder to make political compromises and create good public policy."[53] Extreme polarization can lead to legislative dysfunction, increasingly negative campaigning, and even government shutdowns.[54] It threatens democracy, making it easy and acceptable for one party to dehumanize the other, making deception, violence, and the use of undemocratic methods more likely.[55]

Our government may be polarized, but it's important to remember that the public has voted these divisive, polarizing politicians in. The public has played a crucial role in the extreme polarization of the current political system, whether we would like to admit it or not. There is intense, sometimes violent, partisanship in our elections, and many Americans believe that "the differences between them (political parties) are about more than just politics and policies." [56] Members of one political party believe that the other side's victory would cause permanent damage to America.[57]

These current levels of political polarization can be attributed to many different factors - historical, cultural, and regional divides, a shift of political ideologies, the upsurge of partisan media, and the rise of social media.[58]

Social Media

Social media is a prominent topic in connection to the political ambition of American youth. Young people use social media in place of traditional news sources; most young people learn about current events, social movements, and political news from social media platforms.[59] Social media has powerfully influenced politics, especially how the public perceives the political system.[60] And while social media is not the root cause of political polarization, it contributes to and intensifies it.[61]

The era of social media began with the rise of the internet in the 1990s, followed by the rise of social media platforms, such as Facebook, Twitter, and Instagram, in the early 2000s.[62] The evolution of social media "from platforms facilitating networks among friends to powerful political tools" [63] was solidified during the 2008 election cycle. Over the past two decades, there has been a shift from traditional mass media, such as TV and print newspapers, to digital sources, from online news sites to social media platforms.[64] These shifts have led to the prominence of social media and the prominence of the dangers that come with it.

Social media has drastically changed the political game, both positively and negatively. Social media platforms differ from other forms of digital media (i.e., online newspapers or magazines) due to their ability to host interactions between users and form groups of like-minded individuals.[65] However, this is a double-edged sword. On the one hand, social media can reduce some of the barriers to politics by acting as a cheap and effective source of campaign advertising and allowing political information to be made available to larger amounts of people.[66] Social media has been responsible for the success of several recent social movements, such as the Black Lives Matter movement and the #MeToo movement.[67]

On the other hand, the accessibility of social media makes it easy for creators to manipulate information, especially information that is viewed by younger, easily influenced audiences.[68] Propaganda and misinformation can spread like wildfire on social media, and fact-checkers can't always take it down in time or at all.[69] Divisive content can quickly go viral, fueled by conflict between those who agree and those who disagree with that content.

The accessible nature of social media also enables political figures to interact directly with the public and other politicians. This feature can be beneficial as it can allow public figures to connect with the people they represent. However, it can also be abused, in the example of Donald Trump, who used Twitter to attack other public figures, spread divisive information, and distract the public's attention from policy, law, and national news through controversial tweets that received national press attention from both his supporters and critics.[70]

As for the polarizing nature of social media, it is social media's design itself that promotes political polarization. Social media platforms use an algorithm to maximize user engagement and profits.[71] Social media platforms gather excessive data on their users, from age, gender, race, and location to political identity.[72] These platforms also collect data on user behavior by tracking the content that users have previously viewed or liked.[73] The algorithm uses this data to predict which content users are most likely to engage with.[74] Often, this is content from like-minded users that already matches and supports a user's beliefs, including their political ones.[75] The algorithm prevents social media users from experiencing the diversity of political ideas present in real life. Most of the political ideas expressed on social media platforms are the polar ideological extremes, while centrist and impartial views are few and far between.[76]

This divided concentration of political views does not accurately reflect reality. It can increase incivility and polarization by forcing users to side with one of two political extremes rather than considering more productive views.[77] Social media and partisan media sources (such as Fox News and CNN) paint a picture of an extremely divided America.[78] While there is intense polarization in the United States, Americans are closer in their political beliefs than the media portrays.[79] Most Americans *do* see hyper-partisanship as a problem, with many wanting "their preferred candidate, if elected...(to) focus on addressing the needs of all Americans" rather than on their party's goals only.[80] However, social media distorts the reality of the political spectrum into two opposing forces, contributing to the extreme polarization of America.

It is important to reiterate that social media *has* positively impacted political ambition. Social media has allowed the political world to become more accessible and has been effectively used to engage and encourage young people politically. The polarization of content increases hyper-partisanship, not social media as a whole. Social media is an accessible source of political news and information, but it's important to remember to consume this content with a grain of salt. Always look for reliable sources to fact-check information, fully educate yourself on topics, and form your own opinions and ideas.

The first step towards changing anything is understanding it. This statement, of course, applies to low political ambition. To summarize this chapter, political ambition is formed by one's perceptions of the government. Those perceptions construct one's assessment of the costs and benefits of running for office, i.e., their political ambition. If the costs outweigh the rewards, this results in low political ambition, i.e., a low likelihood that someone will seriously consider running for office. However, when one believes that holding a position of elected office is an effective and efficient way to create positive change, their political ambition increases considerably, so much so that one can overlook the costs of running. Unfortunately, due to their low political exposure and the extreme polarization of the political system, young people do not believe that politics are effective, resulting in dangerously low levels of political ambition.

3

The Gender Gap in Political Ambition

The previous chapter discussed young Americans' low levels of political ambition, but these low levels are not equal. Young women are much less likely to consider running for office than men of similar demographics (age, background, income, and education).[81] Overall, there is about a 16-point percentage gap between men and women's political ambition.[82]

This gender gap in political ambition is present regardless of race, political party affiliation, profession, annual household income, or parental status.[83] As previously mentioned, the underrepresentation of women in political office is because women are less likely to run for office than men. Understanding the reasons behind the gender gap in political ambition is necessary for amending that gap and ensuring equal representation in our political system.

It's important to note that women have unequal political ambition but not unequal ambition. Young women and men are equally likely to desire career success financial success and just as likely to want to improve their communities and the world around them, but men are far more likely to see politics as a way to achieve these goals.[84] As Shauna L. Shames notes in her 2017 book *Out of the Running*, "Young people, women, and people of color are hardly genetically averse to politics; rather these groups led the major social movements of the twentieth century." [85] Women *do* have the desire to create change but do not see politics as a place for them to do so.

There are several reasons for the gender gap in political ambition. This chapter will discuss three main reasons - the added cost of running for office that women see, the process of gender-political socialization, and the phenomenon of self-objectification.

The Added Cost

The first reason calls back to the cost-benefit analysis of politics discussed in the previous chapter. To recap, one's political ambition is determined by an individual's analysis of the costs and benefits that accompany a political candidacy. However, women see higher costs and fewer rewards.[86]

Women see a deterrent that men (at least straight white men) don't see: bias. Women anticipate that they face bias based on their gender, bias in voting, fundraising, and media coverage. Women *do* encounter gender bias in the political system, especially in media coverage, but female potential candidates expect there to be much more bias than there really is. Much of the bias present is unconscious bias rather than explicit bias. Unconscious bias, also called implicit bias, describes the attitudes and beliefs that influence one's behavior without conscious awareness. However false these perceptions of bias may be, they negatively political ambition. If a person believes they will face bias, negativity, or hostility by participating in the political system, they will avoid participating in that system. Women don't want to be involved in a system they believe is pitted against them.

Gender-Political Socialization

The second reason for the gender gap in political ambition is the process of gender-political socialization. Gender-political socialization is the intersection of two processes: gender socialization and political socialization.[87] Socialization is the "process of learning to behave in a way that is acceptable to society." [88] Gender socialization is the process where children learn about and then internalize gender roles and expectations.[89] Society implicitly highlights certain traits as stereotypically masculine and certain as stereotypically feminine.[90] This gendering of traits and roles is present in advertising, film, television, games, school curricula, and personal experiences.

Political socialization is the process by which children are increasingly exposed to politics as they age. Through this political exposure, they gradually develop more complex political ideas and perceptions.[91] These political ideas and perceptions form a person's cost-benefit analysis of running for office, determining their political ambition. Political socialization and gender socialization are both conveyed through the media, family, peers, schools, and interpersonal encounters. [92]

The combination of these two processes creates gender-political socialization - a process that has a huge impact on women's political ambition. Gender socialization teaches children that roles, traits, and characteristics are gendered, and in order to be accepted in society, children must adopt the roles and traits associated with their gender.[93] Much of this socialization is implicit but still powerful. Ideas of traditional gender roles are much more subtle than in the past, but they are still present. Political socialization highlights the traits necessary for political success, traits such as confidence, competition, aggression, and assertion. These traits, necessary for political success, are also stereotypically masculine traits.[94] (Figure 2.1) gender-political socialization paints politics as male-dominated, and stereotypically feminine traits and roles clash with the stereotypically masculine domain of politics.[95] As children age and are exposed to politics and gender expectations, this mismatch causes them to unconsciously view politics as male-dominated - a career for men, not women.[96]

Stereotypically Masculine Traits	Stereotypically Feminine Traits
- Competitive	- Passive
- Assertive	- Nurturing
- Power-seeking	- Emotional
- Stoic	- Dependent
- Aggressive	- Sensitive
- Independent	- Weak
- Strong	- Humble
- Confident	- Cooperative*
- Protective*	- Collaborative*

*These traits aren't necessarily bad/undesirable for politics but in the current hostile political environment, these communal traits are not prioritized.

Figure 2.1

Not only are boys/men socialized to be confident, assertive, aggressive, and competitive (all desirable political traits), but cultural attitudes tell women it is not acceptable or desirable for them to have those same characteristics.[97] Women and girls are often deterred from expressing their opinions and thoughts out of fear of being called "a know-it-all", socialized to apologize before speaking, and taught to diminish their own value.[98] It's been found that men tend to overestimate their abilities while women underestimate theirs.[99]

Through gender-political socialization, girls learn that political roles, roles of leadership, and power conflict with their gender expectations. As they age and are exposed to more and more politics and society's gender expectations, young girls' political ambition decreases dramatically.[100] At young ages, there is not a gender gap in political ambition but "as girls learn more about politics and internalize society's expectations for them, they are less likely to see traditional politics as a place for them to lead" [101] and a gender gap emerges.

Gender-political socialization directly impacts the political ambition of young girls and women, but there are also indirect impacts. All children experience the process of gender-political socialization as they receive more exposure to politics and more exposure to prescribed gender roles and traits. Encouragement from parents and relatives, experience with politics in school or with friends, and participation in competitive activities are all factors that can increase political ambition.[102] However, due to the unconscious societal belief that politics and political traits clash with girls' assigned gender roles, young women are less likely to receive encouragement to run for office - from anyone.[103] There is an extremely strong correlation between being asked to run for office and seriously considering running.[104] This lack of political encouragement is detrimental to young girls' political ambition.

Young men are also more likely to have played organized

competitive sports than young women - likely due to socialization against women being competitive.[105] Gender-political socialization also influences public perception of female candidates. Women who have sought political power have often had to balance gender expectations with political traits, having to balance traditionally masculine political qualities and desirable feminine qualities.[106] This role strain - stress caused when one cannot meet the demands of their social roles - has been linked to worsened health and quality of life.[107] Overall, gender-political socialization negatively impacts women's political ambition, both directly and indirectly.

Self-Objectification

The third reason for women's lower political ambition is the phenomenon of self-objectification. First off, what is self-objectification? What is objectification? *Objectification* is the lowering of a person to the status of an object, and *self-objectification* is when the objectifying gaze is turned inwards on oneself, and objectification is internalized.[108] Constant criticism of and fixation on one's appearance are two common manifestations of self-objectification.[109]

Women have much higher rates of self-objectification than men due to the normalization of female objectification in society.[110] Women are continuously portrayed as just bodies or objects in popular culture. Skinny, attractive female bodies are associated with success and power, suggesting that any body that differs from that ideal is lesser than.[111] The objectification of the female body is spread by the media and consumer culture. In advertising, women's bodies are used to sell products and are thus seen as products for the male consumer to consume.[112] Consumer culture calls for the "commodification of everything and everyone"[113] and it's easy for the female body to be sexualized and commercialized.

Female objectification has always been present in advertising, but it took on a new form with the rise of the internet in the 1990s.[114] The internet allowed an increase in mainstream advertising and an increase in those advertisements' reach. The rise of social media, in-site advertisements, and 24/7 cable news have allowed for increased consumption of advertising - for everyone.[115]

So, self-objectification is much more impactful to women than men, but what does this mean? Self-objectification has many negative effects. It can lead to depression, anxiety, eating disorders, and feelings of shame and inadequacy.[116] Self-objectification also leads to self-surveillance: the constant monitoring of one's appearance. This self-surveillance can diminish cognitive functioning since part of one's cognitive attention is dedicated to body monitoring.[117] Self-objectification is also connected to lower levels of self-confidence and lower levels of personal efficacy; one's belief in one's own abilities. Higher levels of personal efficacy are associated with more success and happiness in school, career, and life in general.[118] But when one self-objectifies, it can cause one to withdraw from engaging in activities and can impair their academic success, relationships,[119] and their ability to reach their fullest potential.[120] Self-objectification is detrimental to personal efficacy.

Personal efficacy and political efficacy are deeply connected as both have to do with one's belief in their abilities; political efficacy is specifically about one's belief one can influence the political system.[121] Self-objectification is detrimental to the self-confidence one needs to even consider running for office.[122] It is detrimental to political efficacy, to one's belief in their own political merit.[123]

To amend the gender gap, one must first become aware of it. This chapter attempts to assist this process by detailing the nature, the causes, and the consequences of this subtle yet powerful gap in political ambition.

The gender gap in political ambition is nuanced. It is also dangerous. Women are less likely to express interest in a political candidacy and therefore less likely to run for office. When women do not run for office, they aren't elected. And when women aren't elected, their voices aren't heard. Their concerns are brushed aside.[124] When young girls look at the political system, a system with few women present, they don't see themselves represented. They don't believe that politics are an option for them. The cycle repeats[125], and it will repeat until measures are taken to end it.

4

The Solutions

Political ambition is not set in stone. It is malleable and can evolve and change as a person grows older, has new experiences, and is exposed to different ideas and people.[126] Currently, the majority of young people have no desire or interest to run for any form of political office at any point in their futures. *But this can be changed.*

This final chapter will highlight some of the solutions that can help amend both the lack of political ambition and the gender gap in political ambition. These solutions will range from being aimed at young people, offering advice to enter the political world and be present and engaged in politics, to highlighting ways that parents, teachers, the media, and the government as a whole can increase political ambition and close the gender gap.

The media we consume makes it easy to view politics as pointless. It's portrayed as a broken system, an undesirable system to be involved in. Our political system is not perfect. Politics are difficult, they are messy, they are sometimes complicated, frustrating, and downright unfair. They are also important and powerful, whether they seem that way or not.

There is a belief that politics are inherently awful, negative, and worthless, a belief that I have heard from my parents, my classmates, and my peers. But this is a misconception. It is not politics themselves that are terrible. The concepts, the values that American politics encapsulate; values of freedom, democracy, and compromise are not inherently bad, they are simply human virtues. It is the polarization, the hostility, the negativity of campaigns, of politicians, and of the media that is bad, *not* the nature of politics itself.

Politics are *power*. Political decisions impact everyone, every day. When people do not speak up, get involved, or run for office, they have no say in the decisions that will ultimately affect them. When young voices, women's voices, and voices of color are not involved or represented, the issues and concerns of a large percentage of the population will not be addressed or considered.[127] The American political system may be broken and corrupt at times, but it is still one of the systems that the United States depends on. And it will not improve without passion and determination, without the hard work of individuals who have the courage to step forward and be involved in the political system in any way they can.

Politics are an opportunity to make change, to contribute to society, and to make a meaningful difference. Being involved in politics, taking a stand, and running for office can inspire and encourage others to do the same, creating a tidal wave of positive change.[128]

It is one thing to ask what you can do for politics but another to ask what can politics do for you. Politics can improve the world but they can also improve the people who are involved in them. Politics can be incredibly rewarding. Political roles, leadership roles, and activism can teach you about yourself, your skills and powers, and about compassion, human nature, and problem-solving. Many people, especially girls, and women, believe that their lack of experience or knowledge of politics prevents them from entering the political world or becoming political activists. They think that they need to be an expert on political issues and processes to participate, but that isn't the case. Getting involved in politics in any way (no matter how big or small) is the first step towards learning and becoming more knowledgeable about politics and the political system.[129]

Change, especially political change, takes time and work. There are many entry points into the political system, points in which anyone can get involved. Not everyone is able to put aside the time, money, and energy required to run for office but there are many ways that anyone (at any age) can contribute to improve their communities and their world. Successful, effective politicians are not born that way, they are not born instantly proficient at public speaking, fundraising, or debate. It takes time to develop those skills and with practice and determination, anyone can do it. Anyone can be a politician, anyone can run for office, whether it be local, state, or federal. The more diverse our system is, the better it functions and the better it represents the public.[130]

The majority of young people express some interest in improving their communities, either as a future career, a pastime, or a non-specific goal.[131] But for teenagers, it can be hard to consider a *career* in politics, whether that be running for office or working behind the scenes. Most teenagers don't even know what they want to be when they grow up. Politics can be overwhelming, especially when you're young, but there are a number of stepping stones into the political world. Participating in sports and extracurricular activities, from soccer teams to book clubs, can improve confidence, develop social skills, expand horizons, and teach young people about competition and teamwork – all skills necessary for politics and for career success in general.[132] For those who are already politically inclined, involvement in student councils or debate teams can be positive political experiences, while taking on or running for leadership positions in clubs and athletics can foster confidence in leadership settings.

> It's important to remember when running for office, whether it's a student council seat, a school board seat, or the highest levels of political office, failure happens. Sometimes you lose, especially when you are young and inexperienced. It's important not to allow failure to define you or stop you from pursuing something you are passionate about. Failure happens to everyone, even the most successful people. People are successful because of their failures, because they experience failure and pushed onward.

Participation in sports and clubs is tied to the development of leadership skills, but there are also ways to be involved in the political world directly. One of the easier ways is to stay informed about current events by following the news – locally, nationally, and even globally. Know your representatives and know what current issues are being discussed and considered. If you're interested, learn about politics by taking a class, reading a book or article, or talking to a knowledgeable person.[133]

Another important extracurricular, not just on the path of political involvement but on the path of personal career and future success, is volunteering. Many high schools in America require students to complete a certain number of community service hours before they can graduate. Even if your high school has no requirement or you've already fulfilled it, volunteering can be incredibly beneficial not only for the organizations that receive the service but for those who volunteer as well. Community service can be a great way to improve your skills, from communication to leadership skills, all while making a positive impact on the community around you. Volunteering can be beneficial for any young person, whether or not they see a political career in their future. And for those who do see that career in their future, there are often opportunities to volunteer for campaigns or as poll workers,[134] These experiences can provide invaluable insight into the political system from a candidate's perspective.

There are many other ways to get involved. As a young person, it can often feel as if you don't have a voice or influence, but it's important to remember that there are many resources and opportunities to create change. If you're old enough to vote, vote! If you're not, encourage those who are to vote. If you find a cause or topic you are interested in, research it and educate others about your findings. If you feel strongly about an upcoming legislative issue, whether negatively or positively, call your representatives and express your viewpoint. It's their job to listen to the public, and your call could be the one that sways their position on an issue. If you find a cause you're passionate about, raise money for it – whether it be to support your local soccer team or donate to an organization that protects endangered wildlife, whether it be with a bake sale or a 5k.[135] There are thousands of ways to get involved, and the key is to find the way that works for you. Use your skills – whether you excel at art, writing, public speaking, or organizing - to find opportunities to speak up, make a difference, and inspire others to do the same.[136]

What can parents do to increase political ambition in their children? Encouragement is the key.[137] Encourage your children to play sports, join clubs, try new things, and find what they're passionate about. Encourage community service and help your kids to find volunteer opportunities. If your child shows interest in law, politics, or activism, encourage them to consider being involved in politics and running for office. Encourage your kids to stay informed about what's happening in the world, and to vote when they can. Teach your children media literacy, the ability to analyze stories in the media and determine their message, accuracy, and credibility.[138] Teach your children their power as citizens and their ability to make change.

Parents can also help to prevent gender-political socialization and self-objectification in their daughters. By encouraging their daughters to act as leaders, to view themselves as leaders, to exercise power, to negotiate, and to take no crap, the impact of gender-political socialization can be lessened.[139]

To prevent self-objectification, media literacy is essential as well as encouragement, specifically encouragement to participate in non-appearance related activities, such as sports and clubs. This can teach girls to value their bodies for their strength and effectiveness rather than just their appearance.[140] To value their legs not for their size or smoothness, but for their power, the power to walk and to run and to go anywhere in the world. To value their chest not for its size but for what lives behind it, their lungs that breathe air, their heart that pumps blood through their body so that it may live. To value their stomach not for its flatness, but for the energy it stores, the food it allows them to consume and then burn as they dance and jump and be. To value their mouth, not for the whiteness of their teeth, but for the words it allows them to speak, the ideas it allows them to express. To value their head, not for the hair on it, but for the mind that it contains, a mind capable of great thought, of compassion, and of anything one could dream of. This encouragement can help young girls grow up to view themselves as effective citizens and potential candidates.

How about schools? Young people spend hours upon hours at school, so how can schools and teachers help increase their student's political ambition? Teaching students how they can be involved in their communities, how they can be involved in the political world, and how they can make a difference is so important. Political encouragement from teachers can also increase political ambition greatly.[141] To combat gender-political socialization, the inclusion of female leaders, both political and not, in the curriculum can evoke the role model effect, encouraging young girls to see themselves represented as leaders.[142]

There are also broader solutions that our government and our society can work to implement. These are more idealistic and unlikely to succeed without time and hard work. To increase citizens' levels of political ambition, the costs of running for office must be lowered and the rewards increased.[143] The political process must be more accessible, with more financial support for candidates, productive media coverage, and fewer barriers to candidacy.[144]

In an ideal world, our government would work more effectively and efficiently. Politicians would act more responsibly and respectfully, and hyper-partisan polarization would end.

Currently, this isn't happening, but with work and time, it

can. Only then can it be shown that politics are an effective and meaningful way to make change. Only then will levels of political ambition rise. Only then will the gender gap in political ambition end. Only then will true equality and true democracy be achieved in the American government.

Politics can be transformative, politics can be beautiful, and politics can be effective but change must be made. Change takes time, but every time someone steps up, change happens, little by little. Everyone is capable of change, capable of changing themselves and of changing the world. There is hope for us yet.

Bibliography

Works Cited

Barrett, Paul, Justin Hendrix, and Grant Sims. 2021. "How Tech Platforms Fuel U.S. Political Polarization and What Government Can Do about It." Brookings. September 27, 2021. https://www.brookings.edu/articles/how-tech-platforms-fuel-u-s-political-polarization-and-what-government-can-do-about-it/.

Bay Atlantic University. 2022. "How to Get into Politics: 7 Ways." Bay Atlantic University. July 28, 2022. https://bau.edu/blog/getting-into-politics/.

Bean, Abby. 2019. "Nasty Woman: Hillary Clinton's Media Coverage and Choices in the 2016 Presidential Election." *Women Leading Change: Case Studies on Women, Gender, and Feminism 4* (1). https://www.google.com/url?q=https://journals.tulane.edu/ncs/article/view/2412&sa=D&source=docs&ust=16956081701311888&usg=AOvVaw23Y6oO1yaWwqMvj2bCm5PX.

Booth, Ruby Belle. 2023. "Youth Are Interested in Political Action, but Lack Support and Opportunities." Circle.tufts.edu. January 30, 2023. https://circle.tufts.edu/latest-research/youth-are-interested-political-action-lack-support-and-opportunities.

Bos, Angela L., Jill S. Greenlee, Mirya R. Holman, Zoe M. Oxley, and J. Celeste Lay. 2021. "This One's for the Boys: How Gendered Political Socialization Limits Girls' Political Ambition and Interest." *American Political Science Review* 116 (2): 1–18. https://doi.org/10.1017/s0003055421001027.

Center For American Women And Politics. 2022. "Milestones for Women in American Politics." Cawp.rutgers.edu. 2022. https://cawp.rutgers.edu/facts/milestones-women-american-politics.

Chan, Katherine. 2023. "Self-Objectification in Women." Verywell Mind. May 8, 2023. https://www.verywellmind.com/what-is-self-objectification-5441926#:~:text=A%20sign%20of%20self%2Dobjectification.

Dimock, Michael, and Richard Wike. 2021. "America Is Exceptional in Its Political Divide." Pew.org. March 29, 2021. https://www.pewtrusts.org/en/trust/archive/winter-2021/america-is-exceptional-in-its-political-divide.

Fox, Richard L., and Jennifer L. Lawless. 2014. "Uncovering the Origins of the Gender Gap in Political Ambition." *American Political Science Review* 108 (3): 499–519. https://doi.org/10.1017/s0003055414000227.

Ghosh, Dipayan. 2020. "Social Media and Politics: Towards Electoral Resilience." *In Resilience*, 2020.

Heldman, Caroline, and Michael Cahill. 2007. "The Beast of Beauty Culture: An Analysis of the Political Effects of Self-Objectification."

Hurst, Victoria. 2014. "The Impact of Self-Objectification on Political Efficacy: Does Self- the Impact of Self-Objectification on Political Efficacy: Does Self- Image Affect Feelings of Political Adequacy Image Affect Feelings of Political Adequacy." https://scholarworks.uni.edu/cgi/viewcontent.cgi?referer=&httpsredir=1&article=1114&context=hpt.

Inter-Parliamentary Union. 2023. "Monthly Ranking of Women in National Parliaments." Parline: The IPU's Open Data

Platform. 2023. https://data.ipu.org/women-ranking?month=7&year=2023.

"January 6 United States Capitol Attack." 2023. Wikipedia. June 14, 2023. https://en.wikipedia.org/wiki/January_6_United_States_Capitol_attack#Attack_on_the_Capitol.

Jilani, Zaid, and Jeremy Adam Smith. 2019. "What Is the True Cost of Polarization in America?" Greater Good. March 4, 2019. https://greatergood.berkeley.edu/article/item/what_is_the_true_cost_of_polarization_in_america.

Kimball, Jill. 2020. "U.S. Is Polarizing Faster than Other Democracies, Study Finds." Brown University. Brown University. January 21, 2020. https://www.brown.edu/news/2020-01-21/polarization.

Kunin, Madeleine. 2008. *Pearls, Politics, and Power*. Chelsea Green Publishing.

Landry, Alexander . 2021. "Dehumanization Is Threatening Democracy | SPSP." Spsp.org. The Society for Personality and Social Psychology. October 13, 2021. https://spsp.org/news-center/character-context-blog/dehumanization-threatening-democracy.

Lawless, Jennifer L, and Richard L Fox. 2013. "Girls Just Wanna Not Run: The Gender Gap in Young Americans' Political Ambition." American University. https://www.american.edu/spa/wpi/upload/girls-just-wanna-not-run_policy-report.pdf.

———. 2015. *Running from Office : Why Young Americans Are Turned off to Politics*. Oxford ; New York: Oxford University Press.

———. 2022a. "It Takes More than a Candidate: The Invincible Gender Gap in Political Ambition." https://www.law.nyu.edu/sites/default/files/It%20Takes%20More%20Than%20A%20Candidate.pdf.

———. 2022b. "The Gender Gap in Political Ambition:

Everything You Need to Know in 10 Charts." Center for Effective Lawmaking. https://thelawmakers.org/wp-content/uploads/2 022/03/Gender-Gap-in-Political-Ambitions_Report_Final-Je n-Lawless-2022-3-1.pdf.

Mankiller, Wilma. 1998. *The Reader's Companion to U.S. Women's History.* Boston, Mass.: Houghton Mifflin Co.

Mckay, Tanjare. 2013. "Female Self-Objectification: Causes, Consequences and Prevention." *McNair Scholars Research Journal* 6 (7). https://commons.emich.edu/cgi/viewcontent.cgi?article =1065&context=mcnair.

Miller, Patrick R. 2015. "Partisan Voters Treat Politics and Elections like a Competitive Sports Rivalry." http://eprints.lse. ac.uk/61965/1/blogs.lse.ac.uk-Partisan%20voters%20treat%2 0politics%20and%20elections%20like%20a%20competitive% 20sports%20rivalry.pdf.

Nickerson, Charlotte. 2022. "Role Strain in Sociology: Definition and Examples." Simply Psychology . November 3, 2022. https://www.simplypsychology.org/what-is-role-strain-in-s ociology.html#:~:text=The%20consequences%20of%20role% 20strain.

O'Brien, Clodagh. 2019. "How Do Social Media Algorithms Work? | Online Digital Marketing Courses." Digitalmarketingin stitute.com. Digital Marketing Institute. May 3, 2019. https://di gitalmarketinginstitute.com/blog/how-do-social-media-algor ithms-work.

Owen, Diana. 2019. "The Past Decade and Future of Political Media: The Ascendance of Social Media." OpenMind. 2019. https://www.bbvaopenmind.com/en/articles/the-past-decade-and-future-of-political-media-the-ascendance-of-social-m edia/.

Parke, R. D., M. S. Leidy, T. J. Schofield, M. A. Miller, and K. L.

Morris. 2008. "Socialization." Edited by Marshall M. Haith and Janette B. Benson. ScienceDirect. San Diego: Academic Press. January 1, 2008. https://www.sciencedirect.com/science/article/abs/pii/B9780123708779001523.

Pew Research Center. 2014. "Political Polarization in the American Public." Pew Research Center. June 12, 2014. https://www.pewresearch.org/politics/2014/06/12/political-polarization-in-the-american-public/.

Rowen-Delson, Jenna. 2021. "How Social Media Impacts Politics | YIP Institute (Opinion Article)." Institute for Youth in Policy. August 10, 2021. https://yipinstitute.org/article/how-social-media-impacts-politics.

Shames, Shauna. 2017. *Out of the Running.* NYU Press.

Simmons, Lee. 2022. "Many Americans Don't See Their Political Rivals as People. But That Can Be Fixed." Stanford Graduate School of Business. October 17, 2022. https://www.gsb.stanford.edu/insights/many-americans-dont-see-their-political-rivals-people-can-be-fixed.

U.S, Inspire. 2019. "7 Ways for Teens to Get Involved in Politics." Bridge Alliance. July 2, 2019. https://www.bridgealliance.us/7_ways_for_teens_to_get_involved_in_politics.

Wikipedia. 2023. "President (Government Title)." Wikipedia. September 16, 2023. https://en.wikipedia.org/wiki/President_(government_title)#:~:text=United%20States.

Zepatos, Thalia, and Elizabeth Kaufman. 1996. *Women for a Change.* Checkmark Books.

Notes

THE UNDER-REPRESENTATION OF WOMEN IN AMERICAN POLITICS

1   Center For American Women and Politics. "Milestones for Women in American Politics"

2   Shames. *Out of the Running*, pg. 23

3   Inter-Parliamentary Union. "Monthly Ranking of Women in National Parliaments"

4   Wikipedia. "President (Government Title)"

5   Inter-Parliamentary Union. "Monthly Ranking of Women in National Parliaments"

6   Kunin. *Pearls, Politics, and Power*. pg. 131

7   Zepatos. *Women For a Change*. pg. 5, 6

8   Shames. *Out of the Running*. pg. 4, 25

9   Lawless. "The Gender Gap in Political Ambition" pg. 1

10   Lawless. "The Gender Gap in Political Ambition" pg. 1

11   Lawless. *Running From Office*, pg. 6, 18, 21, 27

12   Lawless. "It Takes More Than A Candidate" pg. 3, 12

THE LOW POLITICAL AMBITION OF AMERICA'S YOUTH

13   Lawless. *Running From Office*, pg. 3, 20

14   Lawless. *Running From Office*, pg. 21

15   Shames. *Out of the Running*, pg. 6

16   Lawless. *Running From Office*, pg. 27

17   Lawless. *Running From Office*, pg. 38

18   Shames. *Out of the Running*, pg. 72

19   Shames. *Out of the Running*, pg. 169

20   Bos. "This One's For the Boys"

21   Bos. "This One's For the Boys"

22 Shames. *Out of the Running*, pg. 6, 32

23 Shames. *Out of the Running*, pg. 88

24 Shames. *Out of the Running*, pg. 36, 43

25 Shames. *Out of the Running*, pg. 71

26 Shames. *Out of the Running*, pg. 36, 47, 51, 52 (In her interviews, Shames found that almost 75% of her interviewees felt negatively about campaign fundraising. They felt "revulsion, disappointment, disgust, (and) anger" at the idea of having to ask people for money, linking fundraising with having to compromise their beliefs or morals.)

27 Shames. *Out of the Running*, pg. 76, 77

28 Shames. *Out of the Running*, pg. 86

29 Shames. *Out of the Running*, pg. 77, 164, 166

30 Lawless. *Running From Office*, pg. 7, 101, 106, 139

31 Booth. "Youth Are Interested in Political Action"

32 Lawless. *Running From Office*, pg. xi, 14

33 Lawless. *Running From Office*, pg. 9

34 Lawless. *Running From Office*, pg. 60, 108, 110, 111, 113

35 Shames. *Out of the Running*, pg. 49, 164

36 Wikipedia. "January 6 Capitol Attack

37 Jilani. "What is the True Cost of Polarization in America?"

38 Lawless. *Running From Office*, pg. 45 – 47

39 Lawless. *Running From Office*, pg. 53, 54, 70

40 Lawless. *Running From Office*, pg. 56

41 Lawless. *Running From Office*, pg. 62

42 Lawless. *Running From Office*, pg. 73, 77 (Just like parents, teachers can have a huge impact on their student's political perceptions and ambitions.)

43 Lawless. *Running From Office*, pg. 80, 87, 89

44 Lawless. *Running From Office*, pg. 84 (Traditional political media refers to newspapers and television.)

45 Today, the two main partisan news sources that are often pitted against each other seem to be CNN and Fox News.

46 Lawless. *Running From Office*, pg. 101

47 Pew Research Center. "Political Polarization in the American Public"

48 Lawless. "It Takes More Than a Candidate" pg. 8

49 Dimock. "America is Exceptional in its Political Divide"

50 Miller. "Partisan Voters Treat Politics"

51 Some polarization is obviously necessary in democracy as it is present in the very nature of electoral politics. Polarization gives voters choices and can help unify and mobilize voters. It is the *extreme* levels of polarization that negatively affect democracy.

52 Jilani, "What Is the True Cost of Polarization in America?"

53 Kimball. "U.S. is Polarizing Faster"

54 Jilani, "What Is the True Cost of Polarization in America?"

55 Landry, "Dehumanization is Threatening Democracy"

56 Dimock. "America is Exceptional in its Political Divide"

57 Dimock. "America is Exceptional in its Political Divide"

58 Dimock. "America is Exceptional in its Political Divide"

59 Owen. "The Past Decade and Future of Political Media"

60 Rowen-Delson. "How Social Media Impacts Politics"

61 Barrett. "How Tech Platforms Fuel U.S. Political Polarization"

62 Owen. "The Past Decade and Future of Political Media"

63 Owen. "The Past Decade and Future of Political Media"

64 Owen. "The Past Decade and Future of Political Media"

65 Owen. "The Past Decade and Future of Political Media"

66 Rowen-Delson. "How Social Media Impacts Politics"

67 Owen. "The Past Decade and Future of Political Media"

68 Rowen-Delson. "How Social Media Impacts Politics"

69 Ghosh. "Social Media and Politics" pg. 13, 34

70 Owen. "The Past Decade and Future of Political Media"

71 Ghosh. "Social Media and Politics" pg. 19 - 21

72 Ghosh. "Social Media and Politics" pg. 19

73 O'Brien. "How Do Social Media Algorithms Work?"

74 Ghosh. "Social Media and Politics" pg. 19, 20

75 Barrett. "How Tech Platforms Fuel U.S. Political Polarization"

76 Owen. "The Past Decade and Future of Political Media"

77 Owen. "The Past Decade and Future of Political Media"

78 Miller. "Partisan Voters Treat Politics"

79 For example, the majority of Americans support universal background checks for gun purchases but the media does not portray this reality. (Jilani. "What Is the True Cost of Polarization in America?")

80 Dimock. "America is Exceptional in its Political Divide"

THE GENDER GAP IN POLITICAL AMBITION

81 Fox. "Uncovering the Origins of the Gender Gap" pg. 449

82 Lawless. "The Gender Gap in Political Ambition" pg. 2

83 Lawless. "The Gender Gap in Political Ambition" pg. 3

84 Fox. "Uncovering the Origins of the Gender Gap" pg. 512

85 Shames. *Out of the Running*, pg. 170

86 Shames. *Out of the Running*, pg. 28, 108, 111

87 Bos. "This One's For the Boys"

88 Parke. "Socialization"

89 Bos. "This One's For the Boys"

90 McKay. "Female Self-Objectification" pg. 57 - 60

91 Bos. "This One's For the Boys"

92 Bos. "This One's For the Boys"

93 Bos. "This One's For the Boys"

94 Kunin. *Pearls, Politics, and Power*, pg. 159, 165, 188

95 Shames. *Out of the Running*, pg. 121

96 Bos. "This One's For the Boys"

97 Fox. "Uncovering the Origins of the Gender Gap" pg. 505

98 Kunin. *Pearls, Politics, and Power*, pg. 34, 187

99 Fox. "Uncovering the Origins of the Gender Gap" pg. 505

100 Bos. "This One's For the Boys"

101 Bos. "This One's For the Boys"

102 Fox. "Uncovering the Origins of the Gender Gap" pg. 500

103 Lawless. "Girls Just Wanna Not Run" pg. 12

104 Shames, *Out of the Running*, pg. 68

105 Lawless. "Girls Just Wanna Not Run" pg. 10, 11

106 Bean. "Nasty Woman" pg. 4, 5

107 Nickerson. "Role Strain in Sociology"

108 McKay. "Female Self-Objectification" pg. 53

109 Chan. "Self-Objectification in Women"

110 Heldman. "The Beast of Beauty Culture" pg. 13, 14

111 McKay. "Female Self-Objectification" pg. 56, 60

112 Heldman. "The Beast of Beauty Culture" pg. 10, 11, 14

113 Heldman. "The Beast of Beauty Culture" pg. 12

114 Heldman. "The Beast of Beauty Culture" pg. 4, 10

115 Heldman. "The Beast of Beauty Culture" pg. 10

116 Hurst. "The Impact of Self-Objectification on Political Efficacy" pg. 2, 5, 11

117 Heldman. "The Beast of Beauty Culture" pg. 16

118 Heldman. "The Beast of Beauty Culture" pg. 16, 17

119 McKay. "Female Self-Objectification" pg. 64

120 Hurst. "The Impact of Self-Objectification on Political Efficacy" pg. 6

121 Hurst. "The Impact of Self-Objectification on Political Efficacy" pg. 7

122 Heldman. "The Beast of Beauty Culture" pg. 17, 22, 23

123 Hurst. "The Impact of Self-Objectification on Political Efficacy" pg. 20, 21, 26

124 Zepatos. *Women For a Change*, pg 6

125 Hurst. "The Impact of Self-Objectification on Political Efficacy" pg. 26

THE SOLUTIONS

126 Shames. *Out of the Running*, pg. 169

127 Zepatos. *Women For a Change*, pg. 5, 6

128 Zepatos. *Women For a Change*, pg. 11

129 Zepatos. *Women For a Change*, pg. 29, 30

130 Zepatos. *Women For a Change*, pg. 205

131 Shames. *Out of the Running*, pg. 72, 165

132 Mankiller. 1998. *The Reader's Companion Guide to U.S. Women's History*, pg. 557

133 Bay Atlantic University. "How to Get into Politics: 7 Ways"

134 U.S, Inspire. "7 Ways for Teens to Get Involved in Politics"

135 U.S, Inspire. "7 Ways for Teens to Get Involved in Politics"

136 U.S, Inspire. "7 Ways for Teens to Get Involved in Politics

137 Shames. *Out of the Running*, pg. 68

138 McKay. "Female Self-Objectification" pg. 65

139 Kunin. *Pearls, Politics, and Power*, pg. xxi, 207

140 McKay. "Female Self-Objectification" pg. 15

141 Bos. "This One's For the Boys"

142 Bos. "This One's For the Boys"

143 Shames. *Out of the Running*, pg. 103, 167, 169

144 Shames. *Out of the Running*, pg. 37, 38, 40, 167 (Many other democracies provide some or most of campaigning expenses, seeing them as a part of the government's responsibilities.)

About the Author

Evie Kiehle has lived in Southern Vermont her whole life. She grew up surrounded by books and developed a love for reading and writing at a young age. She works at her dad's used bookstore, Book Lovers, on the weekends. She loves running, cross-country skiing, hiking, baking, and spending time with friends and family. She plans to attend college for political science and hopes to continue writing about her passions.